The Story of Alaska

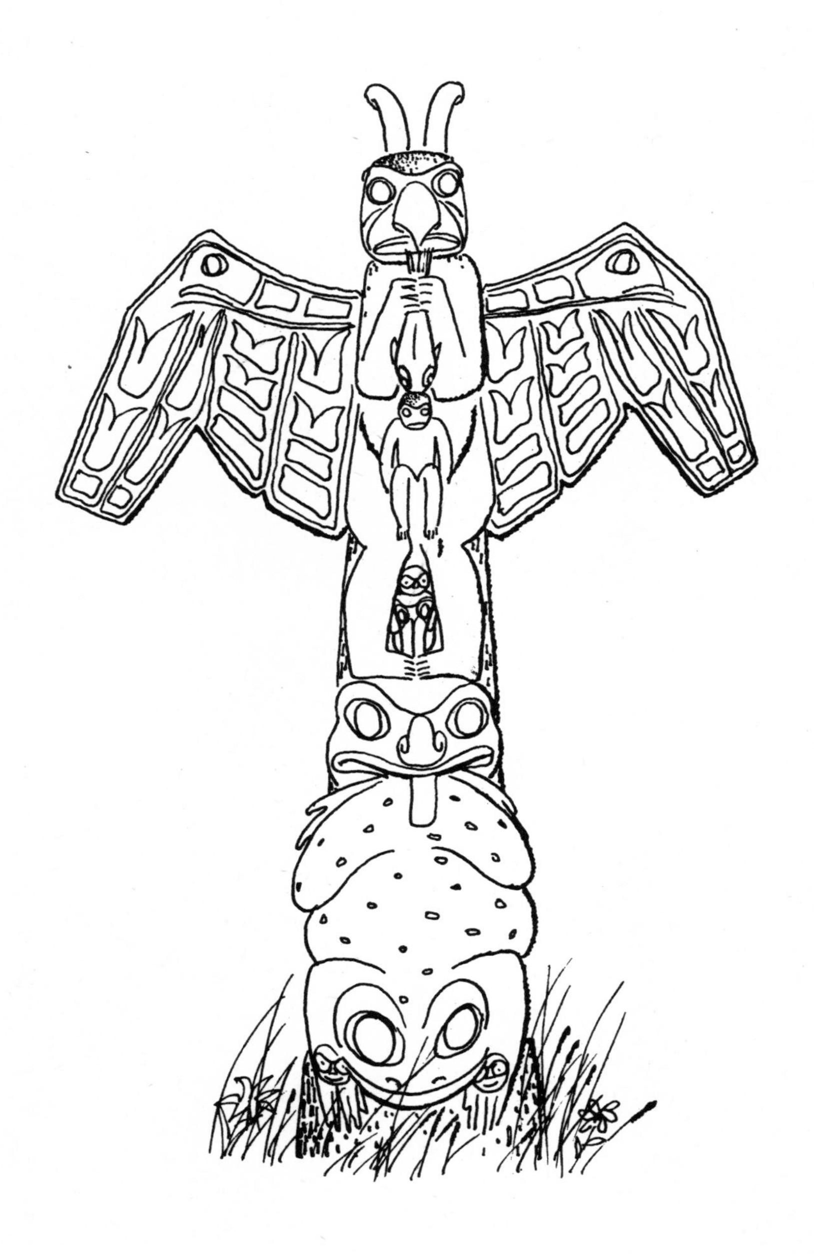

THE STORY OF

ALASKA

By Harold McCracken

Illustrated by Earl Oliver Hurst

GARDEN CITY BOOKS

Garden City, New York

The author gratefully acknowledges the checking of the manuscript of this book by Mr. Al Anderson, Director, and E. J. Huizer, Researcher, of the Alaska Development Board, Juneau, Alaska.

Library of Congress Catalog Card Number 56-6822

Printed in the United States

First Edition

CONTENTS

AL-AY-EK-SA, "THE GREAT LAND"

WHEN the first explorers came across the sea from Siberia and "discovered" the Aleutian Islands, the Stone Age people who lived there told the visitors about a place farther on called *Al-ay-ek-sa*, which means "the great land." The name Alaska comes from this prehistoric origin; although it was not generally used until after 1867 when that vast territory became a part of the United States. For over a hundred years before that time it was known as Russian America—a proud possession of the czars of Imperial Russia.

The story of Alaska is a story of rough and exciting adventure; of hardships, disasters, and riches easily gained from furs and gold.

Alaska sprawls over the entire northwestern part of this continent, covering an area much larger than the combined states of Texas, California, Michigan, Iowa, and New York—about one fifth the size of the whole United States. Its coastline is one and a half times as long as the borders of our country along the Atlantic Ocean, Gulf of Mexico, and the Pacific.

The climate, geographic appearance, and native tribes of Alaska are as varied as its expanse. There are sections where the temperature goes down to 60 degrees or more *below zero* in winter; and other places never get any colder than it does in New York City.

It has the highest mountains in North America. There are many ranges of big peaks, capped with snow that never melts and decorated with numerous glistening glaciers, and whole valleys filled to the brim with ice. Nowhere is there more beautiful mountain scenery.

There are also thousands of square miles of "tundra" or Arctic prairie—flat, and so barren that even the wolves have difficulty in finding enough to eat. Then, too, there are mighty forests of giant trees, where ferns grow luxuriantly high as a man's head, and there are other plants with leaves as large as elephants' ears.

In summer the warm sunshine glows pleasantly upon a large part of Alaska throughout the twenty-four hours of the day, and there is no night. Nearly everywhere, even up to the edge of the mountain snow fields, there is an abundance of beautiful flowers, and ripening berries of many kinds. There are acres of wild lilies of the valley, fragrant as a perfume shop; also roses, purple primroses, lady's-slippers, violets, forget-me-nots, purple orchids, and unusually sweet strawberries.

Everywhere there are birds of many kinds, from great white-headed eagles to tiny gay-colored songbirds; and delicate little hummingbirds, green as glistening emeralds, with shiny ruby throats.

The animal life is abundant. The Alaska Brown Bear, which is a variety of grizzly, is the largest flesh-eating animal that lives anywhere on the earth today. There are thousands of moose, herds of caribou, wild mountain sheep, great gray wolves, wolverines, polar bears, strange walrus, and nearly every variety of valuable fur-bearing animal.

Not all of the natives in Alaska are Eskimos. There are almost as many "Indians," of several varieties. Some of these, living along the rivers of the interior, are similar to those of the northern plains and mountains of our western states. Others, the "totem-pole people," live along the southeastern coast and rivers and are quite different from all the rest. There are also the Aleuts of the Aleutian Islands, who resemble the Japanese or Chinese people and whose origin is still a mystery. Each of these different peoples has its own language, culture, and way of life; its own native costumes, ceremonies, and religious beliefs.

CONQUEST AND FUR

ALASKA was "discovered" by civilized explorers only a little more than two hundred years ago. That is a very short time in the history of the human race. However, the natives who lived on the Aleutian Islands and Alaska Peninsula were still Stone Age people—used only bows and arrows and spears for hunting as well as warfare. Some of the totem-pole people who lived much farther down the coast had learned to pound a few knives out of nuggets of pure copper, but that is as far as they had advanced.

This was before the time when our Declaration of Independence was signed in Philadelphia in 1776—before there was even a United States. Very few English-speaking people had ever been west of the Mississippi River. All but a very small part of North America was still inhabited only by primitive tribes and was open to conquest in the name of any European king or emperor whose explorers were bold enough and strong enough to conquer the territory and plunder the natives of whatever they had that was of value.

The cold northern wilderness areas of the earth have always been rich in furs. Wherever the snowy winters are long and the temperature goes far below zero, the animals grow heavy coats of fur to keep themselves warm. Some of these are soft and silky and beautiful in color—like the fox, sable, beaver, mink, ermine, and the strange Alaska sea otter, which has always been the most valuable of all.

It was the quest for skins of sables that had sent the Cossacks of southeastern Russia roaming across Asia. They reached the Pacific Ocean by 1639, having conquered the whole of Siberia. They were content with the rich fur trade afforded by that vast wilderness until Alaska was discovered.

No one knew how far it was across the sea to America, or what sort of land might be found. But Peter the Great, Czar of Russia, was greedy to rule a more vast empire than he had. He dreamed of ruling the whole earth. He also wanted greater riches from tribute in furs, to build bigger palaces in St. Petersburg.

In 1725 the Czar sent out an expedition to cross the icy sea to explore and claim as much of America as he could add to his domain. As the leader of this important mission he chose a Danish captain who had served in his Royal Navy for many years. The Russians called this brilliant mariner Ivan Ivanovich Bering, although he had been baptized in his native Denmark by the name of Vitus Bering. The undertaking proved to be one of the great adventures of history, although it brought tragedy to many members of the expedition including the illustrious leader.

SEARCH FOR THE NEW WORLD

IT was more than five thousand miles from St. Petersburg to the eastern coast of Siberia. There was only a crude trail across the wilderness, over mountains and through forests, and there were many rivers to cross. Supplies had to be carried on horses and sleds. The winters were long and bitterly cold. Even with all the assistance of the rich czar, it took Bering two and one half years to cross Asia and prepare to set sail upon the sea which today bears his name.

The explorer's first voyage was made with two vessels, the *Fortune* and the *Gabriel.* These small ships had to be built with materials cut by hand from trees on the coast. There were no nails or other metal. All the heavy planks and the boards had to be fastened together with strips of animal hides. There was no canvas for sails, and the explorers had to use tanned reindeer skins obtained from the natives. Thus poorly equipped, they started out.

The expedition moved northward along the eastern coast of Siberia. On August 16, 1727, the two crude little vessels went through what is known today as Bering Strait into the Arctic Ocean. Although they passed within less than forty miles of the western tip of Alaska, they did not realize they were so close to the mainland of America. Later the ships came back the same way without discovering the New World. The explorer returned to St. Petersburg to report to his royal master and to organize a new and larger expedition.

Bering set out again in February 1733 to reach the northwest coast of America. This time he took such a large quantity of supplies and materials and ran into such difficulties that it required more than eight years to carry everything across Siberia and build two new ships.

The expedition sailed on June 4, 1741. The leader was in charge of one of the vessels, the *St. Peter;* and the *St. Paul* was captained by his able assistant, Alexei Chirikof.

They started the fateful voyage from a newly formed settlement in a bay on the Kamchatka Peninsula, which is the most eastern part of Siberia. The place was named Petropavlovsk, which in Russian means "the port of St. Peter and St. Paul." It still retains that name.

This time the explorers sailed southward. They missed the western end of the unknown Aleutian Islands, going blindly out into the great expanse of the Pacific Ocean. Stormy weather and fog caused the two vessels to become separated. Each spent several days trying to find the other; and they finally continued their separate ways. One went on to success, the other to disaster and death.

DISCOVERY OF ALASKA

IT was Chirikof and his crew of the *St. Paul* who were the first Europeans to discover the northwest coast of America. After becoming separated from Bering and the *St. Peter,* they spent a full month fighting the stormy seas, and finally sighted land on the night of July 15, 1741. As daylight came, forest and high mountains loomed before the excited explorers. The great discovery had been achieved. They had reached America, far down the coast of what is today the southeastern part of Alaska.

One of the *St. Paul's* two small boats was sent ashore. It was manned by the vessel's mate and ten sailors. They carried flintlock guns and even took along a small brass cannon; and had provisions for several days. Those on board the *St. Paul* watched the small boat disappear behind a rocky point at the entrance to a large bay.

After several days of patient waiting, Chirikof began to fear that something had happened to his men. Possibly their boat had been damaged in landing. The only other small boat they had was sent, with more armed men to give whatever assistance was necessary and to order the others to return immediately. But none came back.

Another day and another night went by. Then in the early morning there was much rejoicing on the *St. Paul* when two boats were seen coming out of the bay. But it was shortly discovered that these were two large native canoes, filled with hostile savages. They came only close enough to get a look at the vessel; but the full force of the calamity fell upon the explorers. It was now evident that Chirikof's men had been captured—probably all murdered or held for some worse fate. There was also another serious aspect to the situation. Those who remained on the *St. Paul* were left without any small boat to use for going ashore in the future.

Several days were spent in the vicinity, with the vague hope that by some miracle Chirikof's men might return or be rescued. At last, however, it was decided they should return to Siberia as quickly as possible. So the vessel was headed northwest, along the strange coast of rugged mountains and dense forests. Alaska had been discovered in the name of the Czar of Russia; but all those who had been the first to set foot on its shore were left behind—and their fate was never known.

To reach its home port of Petropavlovsk, the little *St. Paul* had to sail along three thousand miles of the stormiest and most dangerous coast on earth. The explorers knew nothing whatever about any part of the mainland or the islands, or the thousands of rocky reefs on which they might be wrecked.

The heavy timbers of the vessel's hull, held together only with strips of hide, were now in danger of being broken apart by each thunderous wave of the storm. The sails strained to hold together against the wind. The food and drinking water on the ship were almost gone.

The weather became very cold. To the hunger, thirst, and exhaustion was added the dread sickness of scurvy and other human ailments. The men began to die, one after another. Chirikof himself became so ill that he could not leave his damp bed. The sails began to tear and the sailors were too weak to mend them. The *St. Paul* moved on slowly westward, with the blind hope of reaching home.

It was little short of a miracle that the vessel managed to escape being wrecked, and finally sailed out around the western end of the Aleutian Islands, turning northward into Bering Sea.

On the morning of October 8 a coast appeared in the distant west. It proved to be the Kamchatka Peninsula. Two days later the *St. Paul* sailed almost helplessly into the bay of Petropavlovsk. The ship's pilot was the only officer who had the strength to stand on the deck. The expedition's astronomer, Croyère, who had been confined in his bed for many days, begged to be helped up onto the deck. But as soon as he came into the fresh air and looked out across the water at the little settlement through his feverish eyes, he slumped down and died.

A cannon was fired to bring help from the shore, and small boats came out to the *St. Paul.* Chirikof and the other ill survivors were carried ashore. Twenty-one of the explorers had lost their lives on the expedition.

Vitus Bering and his men on the *St. Peter*, however, had not returned and nothing was known of their fate.

THE TRAGEDY OF VITUS BERING

WHEN Bering and his ship the *St. Peter* had become separated from the *St. Paul,* the leader of the expedition continued on his quest of discovery. After changing course several times and struggling through stormy weather, he finally sighted the coast of Alaska. His first glimpse of America was the magnificent snowy peak known today as Mount St. Elias, one of the most impressive sights viewed by tourists cruising on passenger ships along the coast. This is several hundred miles north of where Chirikof reached the continent.

Bering's discovery was made on the sixteenth of July, one day after Chirikof first sighted land. These dates and facts are according to each of the explorer's own records of their respective voyages.

Bering sent two small boats ashore. His men found deserted log dwellings and underground storehouses of the Stone Age natives. The Russians took a few of the household articles and some dried salmon, leaving presents of tobacco and other things in exchange.

Bering was exceedingly joyful, for he had spent many long years of dreaming and planning to be the *first* European in all history to reach the northwest coast of America. Little did he realize that his assistant Chirikof had beaten him to it by such a short period of time. But fate was in one sad respect kind to Bering, for he never knew that he had lost the race.

The explorers on the *St. Peter* wished to learn more about the new land and the primitive natives who had run away into the forest when the first boats landed, but Bering impetuously decided to return home even before all the water casks were filled. Strong winds swept down from the great snow-capped mountain, driving the little vessel far out to sea.

It was some time before they could get back to the land again. This was evidently at the large island of Kodiak, quite a distance farther west, but the bad weather and shallow water prevented another landing.

Things began going badly on the *St. Peter* as they set out to find their way home. The fresh water and food supplies had become dangerously low, the Arctic winter was moving rapidly down upon them, and sickness began spreading among the men.

They stopped at one of the islands for fresh water. Here the first of the explorers died. His name was Shumagin, and the group of islands today bears his name on every map of Alaska. It was also here that Bering himself became so ill he could not leave his bed.

The situation became steadily worse. Nearly every day another member of the expedition died and there were hardly enough men well enough to keep the *St. Peter* from drifting onto the reefs or a rocky shore.

It was not until the last of October that the *St. Peter* finally made her way slowly through the western part of the Aleutian Islands and headed for home.

On the fourth of November, land was sighted. There was much excitement and great joy. They hoped it was the coast of Siberia, although no one was sure. The Arctic winter had set in. The sails and rigging were rotted and falling apart. The boat was leaking. The sickness was by now so bad that two sailors had to help each other when their turn came to keep the vessel on its course. When one man became too weak to sit upright and steer, the other took his place as long as he could.

The dying crawled upon the deck to get a glimpse of the distant land, to see with their own eyes what they would not otherwise believe. Bering was carried up onto the deck, so that he too might see the land on the distant horizon. He cried with joy.

The following morning all the ropes that held the sails on the starboard side broke like threads under the weight of the ice that had accumulated upon them. The vessel was completely covered with ice from the freezing sleet and spray. The *St. Peter* became completely at the mercy of wind and sea, and she drifted helplessly.

Another night dropped her black shroud. In the darkness the voyage

of Vitus Bering and his little vessel came to an end on the ice-covered rocks of an unknown shore.

Wrecked beyond escape, the *St. Peter* held together long enough for the survivors to get ashore. Those too weak to walk, were carried by the others. It took four of the strongest to get Bering off the battered hulk of his once-proud ship.

The only shelter that could be found was in small caves dug into the sand bank beside a stream. The open entrances were covered with pieces of the torn sails. Some of the men perished while they were being helped ashore. There was snow on the ground, which the icy wind whipped down from the surrounding hills. Everyone was on the verge of starvation.

Those strong enough staggered out to try and find something to eat—*anything* to eat. They found the carcass of a whale, washed ashore on the icy beach. It had been dead for a long time. But they eagerly cut chunks of the meat and hurried back with it to their hungry comrades.

Many blue foxes came down from the hills. These attractive fur bearers were so bold they came right into the caves and tried to take the whale meat away from the men. The animals had probably never seen human beings, for they had no fear of them.

In a few days some of the explorers became strong enough to go out and try to learn where they were. It was eventually realized they were on a barren island—one of a group that is today known as the Komandorski Islands, named in honor of the "commander" of the expedition.

It was also learned there were a great many sea otters around the island. These richly furred creatures were not only quite easy to capture, when they came ashore, but they proved desirable as food. Even at this

early date their skins were worth as much as 100 Russian rubles, or the equivalent of about $80 apiece in the fur market. Here was easy wealth. The castaways kept the pelts, although it seemed impossible that any of them would ever see home again.

The Arctic winter became increasingly severe, and the suffering was terrible. Vitus Bering held desperately onto life until December 8, 1741. The illustrious explorer's career came to a sad end as he lay in a miserable little cave where the bitter cold could not be kept out, and the sand and snow trickled down upon him. By the tenth of December, thirty-one members of his party had died.

From the wreck of their ship the few who were left endeavored to build a small boat in which to attempt to reach the mainland. Lack of tools made this a slow and almost hopeless task. They decided to call the little boat by the same name, the *St. Peter.*

It was not until the sixteenth of August, after more than nine months on the island, that the few survivors set out on the sea again, leaving behind the scene of suffering and disaster. They took with them more than nine hundred sea otter skins worth a fortune in gold, and a supply of the meat of the animals for food.

Nine days later the tiny *St. Peter* reached the coast of Kamchatka. By sheer good luck they were a short distance from Petropavlovsk. The following day, August 26, 1742, they reached the settlement. There was mingled rejoicing and sorrow among the few inhabitants who welcomed them.

It was the sea otter skins the survivors brought back, more than their stories of geographic discovery, that excited the interest of the Russians. Here was an entirely new source of riches, far beyond the possibilities of all the other furs of Siberia. Quickly the word spread, even back to St. Petersburg. Merchants and adventurers began a race to build boats in which to cross the ocean.

If it had not been for the beautiful and extremely valuable fur of the sea otter, the Russians might not have gone out again to face the difficulties and disasters experienced by Bering's two ships, and Russia might never have ruled in America. But here began one of the most cruel and tyrannical episodes in the history of the human race.

RUSSIAN RULE IN AMERICA

THE explorers, Bering and Chirikof, were scholars in their field and men of fine character. They had with them several scientists of distinction—such as Croyère, the astronomer, who died on the expedition; and Stellar, a world-renowned naturalist, who was one of the survivors of Bering's party. But those who followed them to America were a very different breed of men.

The fur traders of Siberia were known as the *promyshleniki.* They might better have been known as the "fur stealers," for they would not hesitate to stoop to the lowest and most cruel methods of obtaining valuable furs from the natives. They thought nothing of killing a primitive trapper who happened to have a rich catch of fine skins. Most of the *promyshleniki* were descendants of the early Cossack outlaws and plunderers, who a hundred years or more before had roamed out into Siberia. They were very tough and reckless adventurers.

To get to Alaska it was necessary to have a sturdy boat. The materials had to be cut by hand with axes, from green trees of the skimpy forest along the Siberian rivers that ran down to the sea. The fur men knew little or nothing about building a boat. Provisions were scarce and expensive. They were always impatient to get started.

When the crude little vessels put out to sea, there was often no one on board who knew anything about navigation or handling a boat tossed about by violent wind and waves. Even less was known about the land toward which they blindly made their way.

Some of the boats hardly got out of sight of the harbors where they were built before being swamped, and all on board were drowned. Others,

who managed to reach the Aleutian Islands, lost their lives on the rocky reefs, or starved to death, or were killed by the natives. But those who came back were rich men.

One by one the fur seekers reached the islands of Alaska and plied their trade of plunder. From the very first they established a rule of violence and bloodshed. They made slaves of the natives, compelling whole villages of the men to go out and get sea otter skins for them. Those who refused, or did not bring back as many pelts as their new masters thought they should, were brutally treated or killed as an example to the others.

Most of the crude little vessels that came back after a stay of a few months in the Aleutian Islands, brought sea otter skins worth a prince's ransom. One of the first vessels to return brought pelts worth about $128,000. There are records of others that shortly followed with furs that sold for close to half a million dollars! There had never been anything equal to this, and it flared into a wild rush of greedy fortune seekers.

As the Aleutian Islands that were closest to Siberia became known and the sea otters were gradually killed off, the *promyshleniki* moved on farther and farther eastward. They reached the mainland and rapidly pushed on along the coast. Little settlements sprang up where the fur men made their headquarters. Everywhere they ruled the country in the manner which suited their wildest and cruelest fancy.

Finally the Russian government sent representatives to try and establish some semblance of law and order, and to see that the Imperial Treasury got its full share of the fur profits. But a good many of these government representatives became more interested in getting the profits for themselves.

Greek Catholic priests also came to build churches and convert the natives; although, sadly, many of these, too, hungered for the riches so easily obtained.

The rule of the czars became solidly planted in America, although it was completely dominated by the fur men. They did not permit the settlement of the country by persons interested in clearing the land for farms, or the development of other occupations that would in any way affect the natural state of the wilderness. Nothing must interfere with the fur trade.

Headquarters of these rough Russians became scattered along more than two thousand miles of the coast. They were about the farthest away from civilization of any places on earth. Because of this, political and criminal exiles, who had been sent to Siberia, were shipped on to become the first pioneer settlers in Alaska. Being banished to Russian America was far worse than being condemned to the infamous "salt mines" of Siberia. A great many of these starved to death or were massacred by the Alaskan Indians.

As time progressed, the Russians pushed their fur business down the Pacific coast even into northern California. Everywhere they established themselves they ruled the country in the same tyrannical manner.

So intensive were the demands upon the local natives to procure furs, that the animals became scarce in many areas. By about 1850 the sea otters had become so few that it was hardly worth hunting them. This caused the Russians to lose interest in the country.

After more than a hundred years of Russian rule in northwestern America, the United States had become a powerful nation. We had just defeated Mexico and taken California, extending our dominion to a broad expanse on the Pacific coast. The British had moved across Canada. Both nations were challenging the decreasing strength of the Russians on this continent. Even the Czar had grown displeased with the dwindling profits and the manner in which his subjects were carrying on the management of his faraway colony.

Ambitious Americans, now well established in California and the Oregon Territory, began looking with desire on the opportunities of expansion northward. Those who were familiar with the situation had good reasons to believe that, if we did not soon acquire Russian America, all of that territory would become a colony of Great Britain along with the rest of Canada.

So much influence was brought to bear that the Hon. William H. Seward, then our Secretary of State, made a trip to the west coast and up into Russian America, to investigate the situation. The result was that he set himself upon a very determined campaign to induce the United States Government to purchase the entire territory from Russia. This plan was bitterly opposed by many members of our Congress in Washington, D.C., and by most of the newspapers throughout the country. Loud cries were raised, protesting that we should not waste public money on such a worthless expanse of wilderness. It was ridiculed in speeches and lengthy articles as Seward's "Icebox."

"SEWARD'S ICEBOX," U. S. A.

THERE was hardly a section of the earth that was less known in 1867 than the great interior of Russian America. The hostile *promyshleniki,* who had ruled the fur trade along the coast, had jealously protected it from all outside intruders. Most of the great rivers and mountain ranges had never been seen by any white man.

Against great opposition, however, our Secretary of State, Mr. Seward, had proceeded with his plan to purchase the territory from Russia; and after several months of diplomatic negotiations, the two countries agreed on $7,200,000 in gold as the purchase price. The final meeting was held in Washington, D.C., on March 29, 1867, and continued until 4 A.M. the next morning, when the formal papers were signed. Then the proposal went to the U. S. Congress for approval. After two months of heated debate, it was eventually ratified on May 28. The final proclamation of President Andrew Johnson was issued on June 20, 1867. Secretary Seward had proposed the appropriate name of "Alaska" for our new territory—and thus it became known as a possession of the United States.

The actual transfer took place on October 18, 1867, in a brief but picturesque ceremony at Novo Arkhangelsk, which has come to be known as the city of Sitka, Alaska. This was the colonial capital under Russian rule. It is situated on Baranof Island, one of the largest of the group of coastal islands in the southeastern part of the territory, through which winds the scenic Inside Passage so familiar to present-day tourists.

On the appointed morning the American commissioner, General L. H. Rousseau, landed from the U.S.S. *John L. Stephens,* escorted by a company of the U. S. 9th Infantry, with guns polished brightly. They were met by the Russian commissioner, Captain Alexei Pestchourof, who had been appointed to represent the Czar. They promptly marched to the governor's residence, where our soldiers were drawn up at attention side by side with the Russian garrison, on the summit of the rocky eminence where the Russian flag floated at the top of a high flagstaff.

With solemn dignity Captain Pestchourof ordered the Imperial flag of his Czar to be hauled down, making a brief declaration of the transfer of the territory to the United States. It is said that the Russian flag could not be pulled down, and one of the Czar's sailors had to climb up the flagstaff and tear it to pieces in performing his fateful duty.

When the American flag was hauled to the top it hung lifeless. Then, as the two garrisons presented arms, and the Russian batteries and our men of war fired their international salute, a fresh breeze blew down over the wooded mountains to pick up the Stars and Stripes and spread it proudly against the sky. Without further ceremony or speeches or a banquet, this vast area of land belonging by right to neither of the participants was transferred from one European race to the offshoot of another.

There were many Russian tears shed in Sitka that night. It is said that after the ceremony the former Russian governor, Prince Maksoutoff, and his wife retired sadly behind the closed door of their residence, and the charming lady wept bitterly. One proud member of the deposed rulers wandered out into the forest away from the town to avoid seeing the Imperial flag pulled down. "I cannot watch the death of my country," he explained.

"Seward's Icebox" thus became Alaska, U. S. A. All the gates were now thrown open to the full development of all the country's natural resources. A new era of adventure and quest for easy riches was begun.

BROKEN PIECES OF IMPERIAL EMPIRE

THE new Alaska began to blossom in the fall of 1867, very shortly after the American flag was raised over the old Russian fort at Sitka.

Ships flying the Stars and Stripes came from San Francisco and faraway New York. They brought the interesting assortment of human beings who are always drawn to a new frontier, where opportunities are the free privilege of anyone who can find or take them.

New stores, restaurants, warehouses, and cheap hotels were built. Vacant lots in Sitka were staked out, with little regard as to who had been their previous owners; frame shanties were erected; and the property changed hands at prices which promised to make the one street of the picturesque little capital worth as much as the whole territory had cost. Sitka became a boom town.

Some of those who came to Alaska had well-founded ideas about what they wanted to do. There were those with substantial financial backing to develop the rich commercial fishing, or to become engaged in mining projects, or fur trading. There were experienced prospectors from the gold fields of California, merchants from Manhattan, politicians, and gamblers. But most were just restless drifters, with little more than an eager desire to grab any opportunity they might find.

Some of the Americans came into the new territory on ships that never saw Sitka. Among these were the commercial fishermen. Extensive commercial fishing has always been considered one of the most substantial sources of wealth. Alaska was particularly rich in this respect. For centuries fish had provided the native Aleuts, Indians, and Eskimos with their main source of food. The number of salmon annually consumed by the natives was at least 12,000,000. Also, there were great numbers of codfish along the shore of the Alaska Peninsula.

The Russians had begun to develop the fishing industry in a crude sort of way. But the Americans introduced far more progressive methods in this remunerative business. The first year our fishermen took close to half a million codfish in the vicinity of the Shumagin Islands, where the first of Vitus Bering's men had died on their voyage of discovery.

The following year more than 200,000 fur seal skins were taken from the two small islands of St. George and St. Paul in Bering Sea; and the whaling industry, previously made so difficult for American ships in Alaskan waters, was now pursued with vigor. During the first four months of 1868, Yankee whalers took $1,661,922 worth of whale oil and whalebone. There was then a fine market for whalebone, which came out of the mouths of the whales and was used for the ribs in lady's corsets and for buggy whips.

Most of the whaling ships came from ports in our New England states and had to sail around Cape Horn at the southern tip of South America to get to Alaskan waters.

Harpooning the gigantic whales was done from small boats that were rowed out from the big ships. This was exciting and dangerous work. They had to row up very close to stick the harpoon into the whale as it lay on the surface. Frequently the sudden flop of its gigantic tail would smash the small boat and kill the men.

Even more dangerous was the Arctic ice into which the whale hunters pursued their quarry. Often the floating icebergs crushed the big ships, leaving all on board who climbed off on the floating ice to starve or freeze to death. In the fall of 1871, a group of thirty-two large whaling ships was caught in the polar ice north of Bering Strait near the Arctic coast of Alaska. Every one of these ships had to be abandoned by their crews, who miraculously made their way to the barren shore, where there were only a few primitive Eskimos to aid them survive from starvation and freezing to death. This was the greatest disaster in all the history of the whaling industry and has come to be known as "the whaling catastrophe of 1871."

MEN WITHOUT A COUNTRY

ALL the sudden surge of new industry and the complete change in the whole manner of life, which was brought about by the transfer of Alaska to the United States, was a great shock to the Russians who lived in the territory. The treaty of purchase granted these people three years to settle their businesses and get out, or remain and accept all the rights of citizens of the United States. Most were mixed bloods, far more Russian than native. Some had royal blood in their veins and the defiant traits of the *promyshleniki.* They had become a race unto themselves. Their family roots were deep in Alaska and they had no desire to go anywhere else. The transfer was not of their choice, nor had they been consulted in the matter. It was only human that they should resent the many strangers who came rushing in with the privilege of taking possession of their native land.

A number of the deposed officials, who had been born in Russia or Siberia, left Alaska as soon as they could. Even many of these, however, chose to remain and adapt themselves to the new situation. This was also true of the Russian priests, particularly those who had their churches in the remote villages where the Americans were least apt to interfere with things as they were.

On the large island of Kodiak, and farther west along the Alaska Peninsula and among the Aleutian Islands, the villages of the old-time sea otter hunters became like tiny kingdoms. Each was ruled over in the fashion which suited whoever was in control. They now owed no responsibility to the Czar and disdained allegiance to the United States. Each community was independent of the others.

The priests, always a power in the villages, assumed complete rule in a good many of these isolated sections of the country. Some became absolute dictators, reaping the rich profits from all the various furs caught by the natives, whose lives and destinies they completely dominated. Many of these communities retained their Russian character to very recent times.

WHITE MAN'S CONQUEST

THE Alaskan natives became the innocent victims of American conquest very much as the Indians did on our western plains and elsewhere throughout the United States.

Early every summer for untold centuries the salmon had been coming up the coast to swarm into the Alaskan rivers. There were always many millions of these fish. They traveled up the streams to spawn their eggs and create a new generation of their kind. Every old fish died where the eggs were laid. But the young fish swam back into the ocean, most of them returning when they were four or five years old.

Each year the Indians, Aleuts, and Eskimos had caught enough salmon to feed their families through a large part of the year. They ate the fresh fish through the summer. They dried enough in the sun to supply themselves and their dogs through most of the following winter.

The American commercial fishermen stretched nets across the entrances to the rivers, making it almost impossible for the salmon to get to their spawning grounds, or where the natives could catch them. Even out in the bays the fish were scooped up in big seines and nets dragged through the water by ships. The Americans built sprawling factories to put the salmon in cans so they might be transported to distant markets. By the use of these new and efficient methods they were soon shipping as many as 5,000,000 cases of canned salmon in a single season.

The natives were thus deprived of their usual source of food. And, as most of the salmon lived only four or five years to return to their spawning grounds, the fish faced extermination in a brief period of time.

In the more distant Arctic regions the Eskimos suffered even more seriously. Very few salmon went as far north as Bering Strait. For hundreds of generations the Eskimos had secured a comfortable living from the whales, walrus, and seals which had always been abundant along the coast where these people lived. A single whale would feed a whole village for several weeks.

The whalers, having flocked into Alaskan waters as soon as the Russians lost their right to try to keep them out, developed new and better methods to kill the monsters of the sea. Instead of a man standing in the bow of a small boat with a hand harpoon, they began using heavy guns which shot the iron-headed spears with far greater power and accuracy, at much greater distance. Some used guns like good-sized cannons, mounted on the bows of the big ships; and the harpoons were not only a great deal heavier, but they contained bombs which exploded after entering the body of a whale. These methods aided in the wholesale slaughter which left the Eskimo villages without whale meat to feed the hungry families or whale oil to use for heating and cooking in their humble homes. The whalers also killed thousands of the walrus for the ivory of their tusks, which was in demand for covering piano keys; and they shot the seals for their oil and skins. Soon the Eskimos faced starvation, and there was a serious shortage of seal skins for making clothing to keep them warm and for making boats in which to go in search of other food.

There were large herds of caribou, or wild reindeer, roaming over the prairie "tundras" which stretched far back from the coast along Bering Sea and the Arctic Ocean. The Aleuts and Eskimos had depended on these animals as another source of food and clothing. But wherever the commercial fishermen established their salmon canneries, professional hunters were engaged to go out and shoot large numbers of the animals for meat. Some of the canneries employed as many men as the total population of several native villages; and the caribou that were killed to feed them soon caused the animals to disappear from whole areas of the country. In other districts the caribou and other game animals were slaughtered to feed the mining camps and the new towns that were being built.

Practically every natural source of food which the natives and their ancestors had depended on for centuries was intensively hunted and killed off by the white men.

AMERICAN WITH A MISSION

IN August 1877, a visitor came to Alaska who was destined to shape the fortunes of the territory and the lives of its people for generations to come. His name was Sheldon Jackson. Along with Vitus Bering, this man will always stand out as one of the most important in the story of Alaska.

Under Russian rule there had never been much attention paid to human welfare or the rights of individuals. The priests had started a few schools, mostly for religious education of mixed bloods, to carry on the work of the church; but there was little more than slavery for all but the cruel masters of the country.

After the United States took control, the territory came under a military government. The Russian schools declined and were abandoned. American development of the country's natural resources brought about an even worse state of affairs for the natives. Even for our own citizens, the rights of individuals had no legal protection. There was really no law in Alaska. A man could be murdered, his property taken by force, and there was no court in which to prove guilt or innocence. The strongest took what they wanted.

Dr. Sheldon Jackson had come to Alaska to see for himself what he had been told was a very bad state of affairs. He was head of the Presbyterian Missions of the Rocky Mountain Territories, and he had done a great deal for the education and benefit of the Indians in the western part of the United States. What he found in Alaska so deeply impressed this honest man that it gave him a greater inspiration than he had ever had before. He determined to devote his life to bringing about better living conditions and better government, not only for the natives, but for all the people who might choose to live in the wonderful territory.

On that first trip Dr. Jackson established the first American school in Alaska. This was at Fort Wrangell, one of the southernmost settlements, where the natives had been struggling to start a school of their own. The visitor used the funds of his own religious organization. Shortly afterward he established similar schools at Sitka and three other settlements in the southeastern part of the country. But his dreams and his plans went far beyond little schools for teaching the natives to read and write.

Returning to the States, Sheldon Jackson set out on an intensive one-man campaign to tell people throughout the country and to arouse public sentiment to demand a proper government and better living conditions for all the people who lived in Alaska. He held public meetings in our leading cities from the Pacific to the Atlantic. He delivered hundreds of public lectures,

inducing thousands of people to write to their congressmen, urging the creation of a proper civil government, with law and order and other human rights for the citizens of the new country. He gained the support of numerous civic and religious organizations, and on repeated trips to Washington, D.C., he went before congressional committees to urge them to do something about it.

Through six long years he devoted most of his time to these efforts. He also made other trips to Alaska, pushing forward his own program of schools and better government.

On May 14, 1884, the United States Government passed the act creating a civil government for the Territory of Alaska. It was signed by the President three days later. This provided for the appointment of a governor, judge, and other officials.

The untiring efforts of Dr. Sheldon Jackson undoubtedly hastened the action of Congress. He also strongly influenced the shaping of important parts of the act. Among these were provisions that "the fisheries occupied by the natives before the days of the white man should always be secured to them against encroachment"; and "for the education of the children of school age . . . *without reference to race.*"

In April 1885, Dr. Sheldon Jackson was appointed General Agent of Education for the Territory of Alaska; and with this official authority he went on to perform a great service for the natives and others who have since made the territory their home.

REINDEER FOR STARVING ESKIMOS

THE difficulties which faced the American pioneers in Alaska were in many respects greater than those in our Old West. By the 1870s the natives were for the most part friendly toward the white man, although the country itself was one of the toughest on earth. As late as 1885 the more than half a million square miles of rugged mountains, dense forests, and barren lands of the interior were still unexplored.

Travel was mostly by native canoes in summer and dog team in winter. It was almost impossible to use horses because of the character of the country and its swift rivers. Wherever the white man went he must take all his supplies with him. The distances were great, the routes hazardous. Even the hardiest of the adventurers had restricted their pioneering to the coast and along two or three of the largest rivers.

The difficulties did not stop Sheldon Jackson, however, in his work among the natives. Long before the hardy prospectors had discovered the gold of the Klondike, this great benefactor of mankind had carried his program of establishing schools and better living conditions into many remote sections of the country. Tens of thousands of miles of dangerous travel were made. Teachers were stationed in places so far from civilization that they did not see another American for months or a full year at a time. These brave men and women first had to learn the native language and then teach the natives English before they could begin the first lessons of education.

Dr. Jackson went into the distant Arctic regions, where his fellow countrymen had killed off most of the whales and walrus upon which the Eskimos along the coast had always depended for food. He found whole villages starving.

The name *Eskimo* was given these people by their Indian neighbors who lived in the interior of the country. It means "raw-meat eaters." They have always been friendly toward visitors and good-natured in spite of their extremely harsh existence, through hundreds of generations in the Arctic barrens. Before they had so many of the ways of the white man forced upon them, they were a very colorful people. They had a lot of ideas about ghosts and spirits that were good or bad.

The most influential person in every Eskimo village was the *angutkok,* or medicine man. There was always a chief, but it was the *angutkok* whom they respected and feared the most—for he was supposed to have control over about everything on earth, from the blizzards of winter and the storms of the sea, to the luck of the hunters and the health of every man, woman, and child. It was as easy for him to make people sick as it was to cure any illness they might have. To bring about all these things he had a strange assortment of "medicines" that were sometimes hundreds of years old and had been handed down from one medicine man to the next. They included such unusual articles as the mummified bodies of rare birds and oddly shaped figures of artificially colored fur and of carved ivory, which were carried about in an ancient wooden box. All that the *angutkok* had to do was hold the proper one of these "medicines" in his hands, do a little chanting and dancing, and whatever he wanted to happen was supposed to happen.

The Eskimos loved to dance and have big parties. Their dances were storytelling dances, in which large groups of participants pranced and danced about in wild rhythm, chanting the historic stories of their famous ancestors and acting out the episodes in exaggerated pantomine. Sometimes it took all night or a couple of days to tell the whole story. These affairs were generally held in midwinter, when they didn't have much else to do, and they were the occasion for feasting and exchanging presents. Often a whole neighboring village would be invited as guests to the party, and they would come for many miles in their dog sleds, all dressed up in their finest furs.

The Alaskan Eskimos never lived in snow houses except on rare occasions when on journeys in midwinter. Then they might build an *igloo* as a temporary shelter. Their permanent abodes were half-underground dwellings, roofed over with a simple framework of driftwood or the ribs of whales, and covered with layers of grass and earth. They called their houses *innies.*

Sheldon Jackson made his first trip into the Arctic part of Alaska in 1890. He found the Eskimos in far greater need of food than schools. The sea

could not be restocked with whales or walrus. It was also quite impossible to feed these people at government expense, as the Indians in the United States had been fed when the buffalo were gone. But Dr. Jackson had another and better idea. He knew that the nomad tribes of Siberia and also the Laplanders of Arctic Norway had for centuries depended on an unfailing food supply in their herds of domesticated reindeer—like the ones that Santa Claus is supposed to use. The land where the Alaskan Eskimos lived was extremely suitable for the raising of reindeer. Why not introduce this method of self-support?

Going directly to Washington, D.C., Dr. Jackson laid his plan before the proper government officials, requesting the authority and funds to establish the domestic reindeer industry among our Eskimos. This finally resulted in a bill being sent to Congress early in 1891. The plan found very little support and was turned down. It was brought up again, about a year later; and was again rejected by our congressmen.

Failure of our Congress to provide assistance did not stop Sheldon Jackson. Once again he found his own way of carrying out a mission. He made a personal appeal for public contributions, through the newspapers in several of the large cities. This resulted in donations of $2,146, with which he set out to fulfill his plan.

During the summer of 1892, Dr. Jackson personally made five trips to Siberia on the U. S. Revenue Cutter *Bear,* purchasing and transporting 171 head of domesticated reindeer to Alaska. He erected some buildings and

employed a superintendent to manage the project, and he brought over some Siberian natives to teach the Alaskan Eskimos how to take care of the animals.

This was the beginning of the reindeer industry. It spread rapidly throughout Arctic America. For the domestic "deer" not only provided a supply of fine meat, but the natives also used the animals' milk, as well as the skins for clothing and sleeping bags, harness for dog teams, and leather for a great many other purposes. The sinew was used for thread, the horns for knife handles and other utensils, and the hair for mattresses.

More reindeer were brought over from Siberia in 1893 and 1894. During the latter year seven expert reindeer herders were also brought from Lapland in northern Europe to aid further in training the Eskimos.

By 1927 there were an estimated 435,000 domestic reindeer in Alaska, and the industry had produced a total valuation and income in excess of $10,000,000—far more than the whole Territory of Alaska had cost the United States.

The reindeer were introduced for the exclusive benefit of the natives, and laws were enacted making it illegal for any white man to own the animals. Unfortunately, however, it was not very long before scheming white men found ways of getting around the law. By 1927 only a little more than half of the reindeer in Alaska remained the property of the Eskimos. Once again the white man had plundered the rights and possessions of a native race.

HIDDEN TREASURE—FIND IT!

THERE had long been rumors of gold in Alaska—of wilderness stream beds richly sprinkled with nuggets. But the Russian fur men had not permitted anyone to go looking for gold. When the country came under American rule these stories blossomed into the light and rapidly spread to the outside world. This attracted a considerable number of prospectors from the gold fields of California, Arizona, and elsewhere in the United States, who journeyed north to seek their fortunes.

In the 1870s the only town of any consequence in the whole, vast territory was Sitka, and that was as far as any of the American passenger and freight boats went. It was there that the first gold seekers gathered, and they began prospecting the nearby streams and mountains. The results were discouraging, but they pushed on among the islands along the coast.

It was not until the fall of 1880 that a small group of prospectors made a rich discovery near the present city of Juneau, about a hundred miles north of Sitka. During that winter the news spread to the United States. Hundreds of treasure seekers hurried north, and during the following summer Juneau became the new boom town. That season $135,000 worth of gold nuggets was taken out of the small stream, and the next two years more than $650,000 was dug out with very little difficulty. They also found whole mountains of gold-bearing rock—which became the world famous Alaska-Juneau, Treadwell and Douglas mines.

Pushing farther on to find new gold-sprinkled stream beds, however, presented two serious difficulties. The mountains along the coast of the mainland rose abruptly like the walls of a mighty fortress which defied

assault. The rocky passes were choked with icy glaciers and snow fields, over which it seemed impossible to carry enough food to survive in the vast unknown wilderness that lay beyond. Nor could the prospectors go even farther on among the islands and into the short coastal valleys, because of the hostile defiance of the natives.

The Indians of the interior had jealously protected their fine trapping grounds from all intruders. For generations they had followed the custom of trading their furs to the totem-pole Indians of the coast, who in turn had traded the skins to the Russians. The coast natives were as jealous of their part of the arrangement as the others. They would not permit any white men to go into the region north of Juneau, which led to the passes into the forbidden country of the vast interior. They believed that the

American prospectors had ideas of trespassing upon their ancestral trapping rights. They could not understand the white man's crazy desire to find gold, for these primitive people did not realize its value.

Determined to get into the north country and to push on over the passes that led beyond, the gold men devised a rather unusual plan. They engaged the services of a prominent coast chieftain who had come to be known as "Sitka Jack." He was quite a character, who had found much pleasure in adopting many of the American ways in his native mode of life.

The gold men sent Sitka Jack up into the Chilkat and Chilkoot country, which was to become the principal gateway to the famous Klondike gold fields. They dressed him up in comic-opera fashion, which was intended to impress his north-country brethren with his importance. He was carefully instructed in the purpose of his mission, which was to gain permission for the prospectors to go peacefully into the desired region. He was dressed in a blue frock coat, gaudily decorated with military brass buttons and officers' insignias. Over his long, black hair he wore an old Navy hat, with an extra amount of gold braid and other decorations. They even gave him a military sword, which he hung in awkward fashion from a beaded belt around his bulging waist.

Sitka Jack was very proud of his unusual garments and decorations, and he went forth into the north country with all the dignity of which he was capable. He gave assurances that he would convince the Chilkat and Chilkoot people that the prospectors were the nicest sort of friends, who had no interest in trapping or furs.

All through the winter Sitka Jack stayed in the upper country. He went from one little village to another, strutting about and giving presents to the most important persons. He loved to make speeches, and he praised the Americans in terms that almost brought tears to his listeners' eyes.

When he returned to Sitka in the spring he made a speech to the white men who had sent him. He brought back good news and boasted what a smart person he was. Everything had been arranged. The white men could now go up there and hunt for gold. The Chilkats had even promised to talk to the people who ruled the country beyond the mountain passes.

Whereupon the prospectors went to the Chilkat and Chilkoot country. The privileges gained by Sitka Jack did not bring the results which had been hoped for, but this was the first big step toward the fabulous Klondike.

STUMBLING ONTO MILLIONS

IT was in 1882 that the first party of experienced prospectors climbed over one of the high passes that led to the headwaters of the great Yukon River. The next spring some more Americans went over the icy gateway and pushed even farther beyond; and it was not many years before the gold seekers had gone all the way down the river to where it flows into Bering Sea.

The Yukon River was a discouraging place to try to find Nature's golden treasure. The almost two thousand miles through which the great river flowed was an unfriendly wilderness. There were hundreds of tributary streams flowing through hundreds of more miles of mountains and forests. It was dangerous country. Summer and winter were a test of man's courage and luck to survive.

By 1896 a large number of prospectors had reached the Yukon country. They had searched far and wide. Many had found enough gold to keep their desire alive. But the *big strike* in the Klondike had not yet been found—and this is as strange a tale of human fate as has ever been recorded in man's crazy search for gold.

It should be pointed out that the Klondike is not in Alaska, as many people believe. This small district takes its name from a stream that flows into the Yukon River about fifty miles above the present Alaska boundary. Although actually in Canada, the story of the Klondike is so closely associated with Alaska and its development that it cannot otherwise be considered.

A good many men had lost their lives in the treacherous river rapids and the bitter blizzards. Some had gone mad in their fruitless search. Others had become so discouraged they got themselves an Indian woman for a wife and just squatted lazily on the riverbank to watch it flow on to the distant sea.

George Washington Carmack had found a squaw named Kate and he had come to be known as "Siwash George." He lived with the Indians and was seldom seen in the company of white men.

In mid-August of 1896, Siwash George was camped with his adopted relatives at the mouth of the Klondike. The Indian name of this little river means "salmon." The natives always camped there at this time of year to catch the big fish that came up from Bering Sea to spawn.

On this particular afternoon Siwash George sat lazily in front of his dirty tent, with his two Indian brothers-in-law, "Skookum Jim" and "Tagish Charlie."

Out on the Yukon appeared a canoe being paddled by a lone white man. The canoe was abruptly turned toward shore. The man paddled with excited energy. Maybe it was another prospector gone crazy. As the canoe came closer, however, the paddler was recognized. It was Robert Henderson, a Canadian Scotsman, whose luck had not been much better than that of George Washington Carmack.

Siwash George was not happy about having a visitor. He probably wanted a free meal and a gift of some salmon. But Henderson jumped out of the canoe and ran. There was a strange look on his face and he began chattering excitedly.

Henderson had found gold—*lots of it*—on a little stream named Gold Bottom Creek. He had come out to Joe Ladue's for more supplies, having left his three helpers to dig more of the yellow metal. In a few days they had taken out $750 worth.

"It's going to be the biggest stampede this country has ever known!" he insisted. Everybody at Sixty Mile was rushing in.

Henderson had stopped to let Carmack in on the good news, so he could beat the others. But taking the squaw-man aside, he insisted that the Indians should not come along. This was for white men only. Siwash George was not impressed. Nor would he go where his Indian relatives could not go with him. So he gave Henderson a fresh salmon, without offering him a cup of tea.

Later the three men squatting in front of the tent talked about what their visitor had said. They knew where Gold Bottom Creek was located. One of the Indians suggested they could go up the Klondike and one of its branches known as Rabbit Creek to make a short cut over the mountain. Even by starting the next morning, they could be there before Henderson traveled the long way around. Why not go over there and have a look for themselves?

At daybreak the three got into a canoe and went up the Klondike for

a couple of miles to where they took off through the timber. Coming to Rabbit Creek, a stop was made to have a little rest. While one of the Indians was building a fire to boil some tea, Siwash George wandered down to the edge of the stream. Scooping up some sand and water in his gold pan, he began swishing it around and around to see what he might find. In a few moments his eyes began to sparkle, and he called the others to come and look. There was more gold in the bottom rim of the big pan than he had ever seen in a pan before. Collecting the gold, he scooped up another pan of sand and water. This time he got even more of the precious yellow stuff.

Siwash George and his Indian relatives debated what to do. They continued over the mountain to Henderson's camp, staked claims there, and hurried back to Rabbit Creek without telling anyone what they had found.

On the return, Siwash George panned more gold than he had before. One nugget alone was worth more than a hundred dollars! The bearded

squaw-man became so excited that he went splashing about in the water, grabbing up the sand in his bare hands, with eyes bulging in their frantic search for more big nuggets. Even the usually stolid Indians jumped up and down.

They all staked claims. Carmack hacked out a crude sign with his hunting knife, and it was fastened to a tree. On it was carved a new name for his creek: *"BONANZA,"* which in the language of prospectors means *all the gold their dreams had hoped for.* Bonanza Creek was destined to become one of the most famous little streams on earth.

Rushing back to their canoe, the three paddled down the Klondike as fast as they could. They hurried on down the Yukon to the tiny settlement of Sixty Mile, to officially register ownership of the claims they had staked.

On the way they met four prospectors, who were the first going into Henderson's place. When these men saw all the gold that Siwash George had found, they headed straight for the Klondike and the new Bonanza Creek.

At Sixty Mile a score or more others were about ready to leave for Henderson's place. But once again the squaw-man caused them to forget everything but the Klondike.

Word of the new bonanza spread up and down the Yukon and back into the mountains. There were no telephones or telegraph, but the news flashed on and on. Everywhere men headed for the Klondike as fast as they could, to get there before the Arctic winter came to lock the great upper Yukon country from the outside world. Those who had been close enough got there. These were enough to stake claims along the entire length of Bonanza Creek, as well as the main Klondike and its other branches. Gold was found everywhere. Many took out several thousand dollars' worth in a single day. One nugget alone was worth more than $2,000.

Poor Henderson and his men had worked as hard as men ever worked. They could not understand why no one came rushing in to join them, never realizing the wild excitement that was going on just over the mountain. Their own ground proved to be a sad disappointment. Even sadder was the fact that by the time they found out about the discovery Siwash George had made it was too late for them to stake any of the rich ground.

That first winter of 1896–97 on the Klondike brought as weird a situation as ever experienced by a large group of men. Everyone who had a good claim dug out a fortune in gold before the 60-below-zero weather arrived. Joe Ladue staked out a townsite where Siwash George's fish camp had been—which was destined to become the city of Dawson. He built a big store. But soon all the supplies were gone.

In practically every shack there were thousands of dollars' worth of gold. The rough miners had it heaped in tin cans and sacks made of tanned skin and worn-out clothing. Even the richest of these, however, had little or nothing to eat. Bearded men who could pile enough gold on their table to break it down were unable to buy even a can of beans, or a warm pair of socks, or a cake of soap. About all they could get was the meat of moose and caribou, which the Indians brought in from the hills. Even wild meat was sometimes not to be had. It is said that one man starved to death in the bitter cold of a winter night, with enough gold in his dingy shack to have bought a swank hotel or a dozen restaurants.

SEWARD'S "LAND OF GOLD"

AS soon as it was possible to get out of the upper Yukon country in the spring, a number of the lucky fortune finders gathered up their gold and headed for the States. The first to carry the news of the fabulous Klondike gold discovery to the outside world arrived in San Francisco on the morning of July 14, 1897, on a little ship with the name *Excelsior,* which had brought them down from the mouth of the Yukon.

There were forty passengers on that little ship. They were a rough-looking lot, with beards and all in cold-weather clothing, badly worn and stained with mud and sweat, but every one of them had a fortune in gold. Many had their pockets filled with large nuggets, just to play with like marbles.

As there was no wireless communication in those days, no one knew what had happened until the *Excelsior* made her lines fast to the San Francisco wharf and the first of the men jumped ashore. Then the sensational news began flashing out through the civilized world.

"Gold found in Alaska! A place called the Klondike! Richer than anything ever known before!" This was the word carried to every town in the United States, and to Europe and elsewhere. The effect was like a declaration of war. The telegraph lines were jammed with story after story. Big black headlines spread across the newspapers and people carried the news from one to another. Men stopped their work to talk about it or to dream up plans of rushing away on a mad dash to get some of the free gold for themselves.

Three days later another little ship came in from the sea. This was the *Portland,* which docked at Seattle. She carried sixty passengers, also from the Klondike, and these men brought with them more than $700,000 worth of gold. Once again the telegraph lines were jammed with the news. Overnight the new name "Klondike" had become the most magic word in the English language.

In every big city and thousands of small towns from coast to coast, and in many countries across the seas, men suddenly left their jobs and their families, to rush to railroad stations and steamship offices. Practically none of these folks knew just where the Klondike was or realized the hardships they faced to get there, but *to the Klondike they were going.* The big stampede was begun.

Many millions of dollars' worth of gold were dug out of the Klondike. There are accounts of $1,000 taken from a single pan of sand, and one man's claim on a tiny stream was sold for $2,000,000.

What happened to Henderson, who started the whole thing, and to Siwash George and his Indian relatives? Henderson sold his claims for a mere $3,000 in gold dust that had been taken out of the nearby Klondike. The purchasers afterward struck it rich, digging out more than a hundred times what they paid for the property. Bitterly disappointed, Henderson finally left the country with only $1,100; and even this was stolen from him on the way to Seattle. He died a poor man.

Siwash George and his Indian partners were all pretty lazy and they didn't dig out nearly as much as others did. What they got they squandered foolishly. In the summer of 1898 George left his native wife and her two brothers to look after their rich claims and he went to the States, where he could spend his wealth in a more exciting manner. All that he took along was soon gone.

In the meantime, sharpsters managed to get the claims away from Kate and her Indian brothers. All that George Washington Carmack received as his share was a mere $60,000. This, like all the rest of the money, was rapidly and unwisely spent, and he too suffered the misfortunes of a poor man through all of his remaining years—although the golden treasure of the Klondike, upon which Siwash George had so strangely stumbled, continued to make hundreds of other men rich.

Where the Indian fish camp had been, the town of Dawson grew like a mushroom into a rough and glamorous metropolis of the Arctic frontier, with streets lined with stores, saloons, hotels, and gay dance halls. The raw gold from the nearby stream beds was scattered about with wild abandon. Some of the characters around town have become colorful legends of the Far North—such as the one known as "Swiftwater Bill," who gave a dance-hall girl her weight in nuggets just to get her to marry him.

Far more fortune seekers came to the Klondike than there was room along the streams for them to dig for treasure. They kept coming by the thousands. They spread out into other parts of the country, mostly in Alaska. Gold was found in many places. In July 1899, a discovery was made which rivaled even the Klondike. This was on the sandy beach on the northern shore of Bering Sea, where the city of Nome stands today. Within three months over 8,000 gold seekers were camped there, and many of the get-rich-quick stories of the Klondike were repeated. This brought many more thousands of people hurrying north. Alaska rapidly became known, *not* as "Seward's Icebox," but as "Seward's Land of Gold."

OUR LAST FRONTIER

THE discovery of the Klondike, which is really in Canada, was the most important event which led to the exploration, settlement, and development of Alaska. The large number of people who were thus drawn to our territory in the Far Northwest pushed into practically every valley and mountain region. Little towns sprang up. Regular steamship service was established to bring in the necessary supplies and mail and more people. Hundreds of the prospectors turned their attention to finding and developing the large deposits of copper ore, which led to the establishment of elaborate mining plants that employed hundreds of workmen and required the building of railroads. The coal and petroleum deposits have led to the employment of many more. Others, who came from the agricultural regions of the United States, settled down to start farms and dairy industries in the new land.

There are of course other factors which have in recent years contributed to the development of Alaska and the steady progress in transforming our last wild frontier into a modern place to live. The introduction of the airplane played an important part. In the 1930s and 1940s, "bush pilots" began flying their little planes to remote settlements and mining centers, carrying men, supplies, and even machinery, and bringing out gold and furs. This is a story of heroic pioneering, and it revolutionized transportation and gave great encouragement to new undertakings.

The building of the "Alcan" or Alaska Highway across Canada and into Alaska has made it possible to drive the family jalopy from anywhere in the United States to the centers of population in the territory. Further road construction has since been spreading out into a network of main highways and secondary roads. In big valleys, where not many years ago the dog team and pack horse were man's only aids to travel, the automobile has come to be a common sight.

Law and order have become as rigidly enforced and respected as in any state of the Union; and government regulations over harvesting the natural resources have insured these for many generations to come. The fishing industry, which once threatened to quickly exterminate the salmon, has for many years been scientifically controlled—yet the canned salmon which has been shipped out in a *single year* has been valued at *twelve times* the total amount our government paid Russia for the whole territory.

World War II brought Alaska into a new importance. This was not fully realized until the Japanese invaded the Aleutian Islands and threatened to take control of the whole northwestern part of our continent. Since then there has been a tremendous build-up of military power in Alaska as a protection to all the free people in North America. Let us hope that those defenses may never be put to a real test, but their building and being kept in proper condition for immediate use, if necessary, have greatly aided in the peaceful development of the Far North.

This vast land of rugged mountains and romantic enchantment has become a favorite playground for tourists as well as big-game hunters and fishermen. Every year increasing numbers of people, from schoolteachers to vacationing families, journey comfortably to the Far Northwest. It is now very easy to enjoy the marvelous scenic beauties and take snapshots of Eskimos dressed up in their ancestral fur parkas, under which they are probably wearing the same sort of clothing as the tourists.

Alaska has been a land of dramatic experience. There is probably no place on earth where so many people have found so much wealth among Nature's treasure.

The territory has seen a rapid parade of remarkable changes. Today it is possible to leave the United States in the morning in a comfortable big four-engined airplane and fly to Point Barrow at the northernmost Arctic tip of the continent, arriving the same afternoon. Only a few years ago such a trip could only be made by boat and was considered a real "expedition," often requiring a whole summer of dangerous adventure. And the Eskimos who live there now order white man's clothing, household goods, and foods from the big mail-order companies in the United States, delivered by airplane. Throughout the territory Alaskans have become the "flyingest people on earth."

In spite of all this development, and all the changes to modern ways of life, the 1954 estimate of the total population of both whites and natives in Alaska was set at only 208,000. That is less than half as many people as live in Albany, New York, and not a third of the population of Washington, D.C.—scattered over an area one fifth the size of the whole United States.

There is hardly a place in the territory where the white man has not been, although large areas remain just about as wild as they were when the natives were a Stone Age people and the Russian explorers sailed across Bering Sea on their first voyages of discovery. There is still plenty of adventure for those who choose to find it—in a northern wonderland where vast quantities of Nature's hidden treasures still wait to be found. We have only begun to enjoy the many and varied benefits which have become ours in "the great land" of Alaska.